# Poems For The Weeping Kind

## By Althea Davis

**Content Advisory:** *Poems For The Weeping Kind* explores
mature situations including generational trauma,
addiction, partner abuse, intimacy, religion, and death.

*A cherished family heirloom, the painting
featured on the cover was created especially for
the author's maternal grandfather by her father.*

For my Mom and Dad. They made me,
and they made me a writer.

For my twin, whom I would give every word to, if they wanted.

For all of the loves of my life, especially the good ones.

And for me, forever the weeping kind.
Forever that little girl with wire glasses
who took everything she ever felt
and made it into poetry.

"'I've had a hard life,
But so have we all.
I've built a collection,
the bricks in my wall.
To share it with you,
who sometimes weep in the night.
In hopes it will bring,
a glimmer of light.'"

-Unknown Author

# On Love

## Peach

I will come to you,
like I have before.
Small and bruised,
the softest peach
from my family tree.
I will ask you to bite into me,
hoping I am anything
but old and bitter.
Let me sit at your doorstep,
just a few more hours.
I will change, I promise.
I could be ripe, darling.
I could satiate you,
if you just wait.
Let me rest here,
in the beginning of our home.
Let me sleep
in this doorway.
Hoping one morning,
I will have a place in your bed.
And we will wake
with our arms around each other.
And eat peaches for breakfast,
perfectly ripe.

## I Am Hers

She makes me complete
on the kitchen table.
Makes me feel like a girl
in the Summer heat.
She helps me stand,
legs wobbling,
slick with someone else's sweat.
I am nervous,
but don't have the words
to tell her why
her hands on me
make me feel ashamed.
I forget all that came before this,
her soft sweet voice,
the creaking table,
stormy skies and humid air.
I forget my name.
So I just take hers.
If I am a monster,
then I am her monster.

## It Was Never Shameful

Tonight
I feel sweet and soft
in all the ways I used to hate.
The beer you gave me
is bitter.
It makes my spit taste sweet.
Your name from my lips
is honey.
It is shameful
how I want to love you.
My Dad is no drinker
but I have another in his name.
Liquid courage
is my father's blood running through
me.
I am brave
as I am his daughter.
She laughs so loud,
and you seem to breathe it in.
It is a soft loving thing,
watching you watching her.
And I am jealous in a way.
Because the way I love you both
feels shameful.
I wonder what my Dad would think.

## Dedicated to a Pretty Girl

If the world was ending,
if it came crashing down at our feet,
I think it would be kind of sweet
to end with you.
If fire took the world,
would you finally let our hands touch?
Ignore the heat on my cheeks,
as my skin melted to yours.
Would you let me call you hot?
As my mother's leather couches
boiled,
and she prayed for snow.
If my mother's prayers came true,
if winter took the world,
would you let me
be anything but cold to you?

Would you hold me,
as I called my Dad and weeped?
And told him I loved him more than any-
thing.
Would you introduce yourself,
and tell him he would've loved you?
I bet he would have.
If it ends in a storm
would you go outside with me
and dance in the rain?
With my twin and all of our best friends.
Splash in the puddles,
like we are children,
and scream
because we never got to have any.
But if we did,
would you let me name them Sue?
If the world ended,
would you love me?

## We Never Did Get Married

And should you ever doubt
the love I hold for you,
I will rip out my holy ribs.
(Like God once did to Adam
though I am no God
and I am no Adam.)
Bend them into a bow,
string it with pieces of hair,
I plucked from your pillow.
And shoot down the moon with it.
When it falls from the sky,
I will catch it in the hands
you hold so dearly.
And make you a pearl ring.
A wedding ring,
made of stardust and the moon.

And with that the universe said,
I love you.

## I'm Still Thinking About You

I imagine my life
a piece of yarn,
stretched and reaching,
between the beginning and the end.
It is thick and red,
like my fathers blood
running through me.
I am his daughter
as I am that yarn.
And I see yours,
parallel to mine.
Star crossed lovers,
nothing but string now.

And though we'll never touch again,
I imagine in another ending and beginning.
Us.
Tangled together,
making new blood and new yarn.
Watching movies and folding laundry.
And you love me,
like you were always supposed to.
And we don't think
about those other pieces of yarn.
We don't think about yarn at all.
We just think of each other.


I'm gonna try to stop thinking about you.

## I Want You

I have never wanted to be anything,
more than I have wanted
to be yours.
To be held in a way
that is anything but gentle.
To have your fingers
bruised in me.
And your teeth
embedded in me.
If I bleed,
I will wear it.
My scarlet letter.
I know you are sweet and soft.
But I'd like to see you hard.
You know exactly what I mean by that.
Let me die in your embrace.
You know exactly how to bring me back.
Your arms around me are heaven.
So let me lie,
in the space between your thighs,
and show you just how much
I want you.

## Coffee

I hope you still make coffee
the way I taught you.
Hope your cup is always clean
and the taste is never bitter.
Hope you find someone
to drink it with.
Maybe they know
how you take it,
and make it for you.
Maybe they even taught you
a new way to make it.
I really hope someone loves you
like that.
Even if it didn't get to be me.

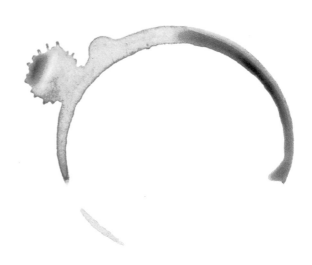

## I Burn for You

It is 1 in the morning.
I was dreaming
that your hands
still called my blushing face
their home.
And my cheeks burned
when I woke up.
Knowing they would never again
be the color you made them.
And it scalds me.
Because I know
even when I die,
and never get to dream again,
my dirty face
will still miss your hands.
Oh God, it scalds me.
Because I know
even when I die,
Hell is just another place,
I would burn for you.

# On God

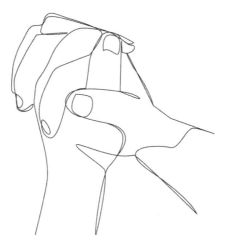

## God's Tears

When I was a little girl,
I fell in love.
I fell in love with a tree.
The way its branches looked like hands,
reaching towards the sun.
It looked as if it were looking for a God.
I was too.
When it snowed,
I would make wedding rings and snow angels for my tree.
I fell in love with rain.
The way it felt against my skin.
Like my tree, I craved the touch.
My teacher told me that the rain was God's tears.
So me and my tree would sit in the rain.
My grandmother used to give all of us children a cup,
and tell us to collect rainwater.
That we couldn't come back until we had a full cup.
We would laugh at first.
Run around the wet grass,
open our mouths for raindrops.
I've never tasted anything sweeter,
than God's tears in the Summer.
Eventually we would get bored
and fill the cup with river water.
How strange it was to cheat my grandmother out of God.
I wonder what my tree would have thought of that?

## Bruised

If I met Him,
He would curl up at my feet
like a dog.
Kicked too many times
in the ribs.
I would lift my shirt,
and show Him the bruise
I have become.
He would kiss my feet.
Whimper and beg
for forgiveness,
I was never shown.
And I would give it to Him.
Stroke his hair and hold Him.
How my father did to me.

(For even when I am gone,
I will remember
the way my father held me.
As all daughters do.)
And I would tell Him.
God.
He did not make me.
And neither did what he put me through.
I am my mother and my father's child.
I am bruised in their image.
The way they were bruised.
And I will forgive him
in my daughter's name.
So that she
may not be bruised,
like me.

## My Brother, the God

Racing through the woods,
sticks and thorns piercing our feet.
We feel nothing.
Nothing but this,
this glee.
Brothers born
of mud and teeth.
Alone in the dark and the stars.
The moon so sweetly
holding our faces.
Like I ache to hold him.
My baby.
The point of his elbows,
and the sharp of his wit,
cut me down to nothing.

Does he feel nothing?
Does the heat of the summer,
we shared as a family prayer,
not scald and bruise him
like it does me?
The mud by the river.
The flowers we picked,
for a mother we shared,
felt religious.
He looks down on it now.
My brother,
the God, has forgotten
we were brothers born
of mud and teeth.
He has forgotten.
We were brothers.

## Eventually, it was the Last Time

He hits me,
for the first time.
And I see God.
I see row after row
of church pews.
My family sits in them.
They look at me,
but none of them smile.
I walk down the aisle,
my fingers grazing the wood.
I think of the tree I used to climb as a little girl.
Was it made into something holy?
Sometimes you have to be cut down,
to be beautiful.

And as I walk that hallowed hallway,
I feel all the good parts of me,
fall to the ground.
I keep walking.
If a girl falls into an early grave
and no one is around to stop her,
to stop him,
does she make a sound?
Does anyone stop to pick up the pieces?
I don't.

He hits me
for the first time
and I know,
God knows,
it won't be the last.

## You Never Leave Me

How to salvage
the unsalvageable?
How to get back thine heart
when it is to yours
like a brother in the womb?
We grew together
and so the God says,
we must die together.
But what if I am not to die?
What if I am to break
thines holy heart
from mine,
and live?
Truly live.
May I be damned
for self preservation?
And if I am damned,
when I get to that awful place,
and it is exactly the home I left,
will you be there?

## He Really Does Forgive Me Every Time

When I was a kid,
my Father was God
in my eyes.
The way he laughed
and threw back his head.
The way he shaved his beard
and the stubble kissed my face.
Like everything sharp and everything soft.
The way he wasn't there,
felt holy.
Even when he was gone,
it felt like he never really left.
Maybe it was because I knew
he didn't want to leave.
He'd toss me in the air
and I'd wonder,
if I would ever fall from his grace,
would he forgive me?
And that's how I know,
my Dad isn't God.
He forgives me
every time.

I feel bad for Lucifer.

# On Trauma

# and Healing

## I Still Miss It

Girl.
All I am.
All I have known.
Girl.
Small and weak.
Pretty and prim.
I curtsy and they giggle.
This
Girl
was not made for this.
Something in me,
came out broken.
Or maybe,
it just ended up that way.

Girl.
Still small.
Still weak.
Not pretty.
I cut off all my hair,
to make myself something else.
Disguise myself.
Hide these hallowed breasts and ugly cunt.
It doesn't work.
They get the
Girl.
He holds me down
and makes me a
"Woman"
And suddenly
I wish I was just a
girl.

## My Twin Hates This One

I die young.
Like my father was supposed to.
Like my mother thought she would.
My twin finds me,
curled in the bed
I was supposed to be only loved in.
And they can't help but scream.
We've got the same bones,
but mine weren't made for loving.

## God is Mean

I am telling all my friends
how I lost the weight.
And your hand digs into my thighs
under the table.
Trying to carve out pieces of me.
I promise I am doing it
just like we practiced.
Sucking in every pound and every word,
that doesn't frame me,
as your perfect girl.
I stand in front of the mirror,
for hours.
Holding my mouth just right,
as I say your last name in place of mine.
(The whole time wondering
what my father would think,
if he knew how much I loved
Althea Davis.
And how hard it is
to have to give it up.)

You tell my friends I drink too much.
So as I carry you to my bed.
I pray it falls in on us both,
and they find the bottle in your hand.
I wake up.
You're on top of me,
and I think,
God is mean.
And I understand
why my mother was a drinker.

## Sharp

You're mean.
Don't you ever forget that.
You're sharp for a reason.
What they cut out of you,
comes back different.
You come back different.
The soft leaves,
and it doesn't come back.
Your mother holds you
and flinches.
She knows her part in this sharp.
When she holds you,
you can feel every part of you she took.
And every part of her you took.
You are your mothers daughter,
and you're meaner for that.
So don't let her hold you anymore.
Don't let anyone hold you.
They will trick themselves into believing you are
something other than you are.
You're a mean fucking bitch.
Don't forget that.
They cut you to make you remember.
So be sharp.
Cut back.
And never forget.

## Somebody's

She says
I don't love her
how she needs me to.
And I am 17 again.
Mother screaming
that I am mean.
A mean girl.
And I think
maybe I wasn't meant to be
somebody's daughter.
And I hold my head in my hands
and weep.
Because though I am 21 now,
I still don't think,
I know how to love right.
I am still mean.
A mean girl.
Maybe I wasn't meant to be
somebody's.

## I Will Gut You

This
is the lesson
you learned.
The moral
of our story.
Though you
on your own,
may have no morals.
I will gut you and me both,
if I need to.
I am honest
to a fault.
I was not made for this.
To fall apart in your arms,
to come undone.
I will not break.
I will remain.
And I will gut you,
if I must.
Tear you with my teeth,
and cut you with my tongue.
I am not mean.
I am honest,
to a fault.
Your fault.
This is your fault.
And your lesson.

## July

I come to you,
that summer evening.
Empty bellied and bruised.
Shivering, even in the sunlight.
I have not been kind to myself.
This April scalds me.
Because I know,
July is coming.
His ghost waits for me there.
As it will,
year after year.
You take me in open arms.
Feed me blackberries and sugar.
Take the sunshine on your cheeks
and rub it onto mine.
Hold me like I am everything,
when in reality I am nothing.
The days will go by,
and turn into years.
And my hair will turn gray.
(Early, I imagine, like my Father.)
And my belly will stay empty,
but feel full only in your arms.
And God, I pray your house
will stay Summer.
Will stay anything,
but July.

## I'm Still Me

Who was I
before it happened.
Younger, I know.
My face fuller,
always colored pink.
Frame smaller.
Smaller.
I was so small.
So young.
Was I sweeter?
Kinder?
I don't remember.
I don't think I'm mean now.
But maybe she would,
that girl who was me.
But I have her veins,
her blood and bone.
I'm still my fathers daughter.
Still have his eyes.
I'm still me.
Even after everything that happened.
I'm still me.

## Life Moves On

There is something so comforting,
something magic,
in the way that life moves on.
Last night while I lay sleeping,
my heart was broken.
I curled in on myself,
even in my dreams.
Trying to make myself lesser.
Trying to convince myself,
I am a half now.
But when I woke,
the ache was dull,
and I filled my bed.
On the way to work,
I begged something tragic to happen.
So that I may hold onto the hurt,
just a little longer.
But it never did.
I somehow equated the hurt leaving,
to the people that made me hurt, leaving.
And that was horrifying.
So I pleaded for it to all stay.
And it never does.
And there is something comforting in that.
Something magic.

On Dreams

## And Her Name Was Sue

I had a dream,
that I had a daughter.
I never wanted kids.
But she looked just like me.
Blue eyes and brown hair,
my same snaggle teeth.
I held her,
the little girl I used to be.
And she started to cry.
Maybe she knew,
she wasn't meant to be a daughter.
The same way I knew,
I wasn't meant to be a mother.
I woke up crying.
Because I never wanted kids.
Yet I still dream,
about being loved like that.

## This One Still Scares Me

I wake up.
And I know I shouldn't have.
The world is quiet.
I leave my room,
and the stained hardwood floors don't creak.
My heavy feet make no sound.
I walk like I never did wake up.
No music plays,
from my mothers hippie room.
The Grateful Dead and Beatles have died,
in a far more final way.
And I hear no laughter,
from my twin's room.
I do not dare to enter.
I know they are gone.

And it breaks my heart.
Because we were always supposed to go together.
I wanna call my Dad.
But I'm scared of the silence, that phone call will hold.
He is always there when I need him.
If he is gone,
it means I will never need him again.
I don't understand what that means,
and I wish I could ask him.
The whole world died when I slept,
and no one woke me up for the funeral.
There are no bodies to bury.
There
is
just
me.

## You Never Did Like Coffee

That night I dreamt,
we were sitting in a diner.
The coffee was hot and sweet,
and my pockets were full.
You watched me pour in too much cream,
while he took his black.
And you laughed
at how different we all are.
Because you don't even drink coffee.
And I thought in that moment,
I love you, I love you, I love you.
And I wondered if you'd like coffee,
if you tasted it from my lips.
I know he would.
I think I'd like to ask you.
But even in my dreams,
I am not so bold.
I wake up.
And my pockets are empty.
But for some reason,
this morning it doesn't matter.
I yawn.
And I taste
coffee.

# The Bumblebees Still Remember You

You were in my dream last night!
We were drinking whiskey and honey.
Your feet were buzzing!
And when I looked in your shoes,
they were full of bumblebee legs.
I laughed, and they danced with me.
I guess we were both a little buzzed.
When we were little,
you used to catch them in your hands,
let them rest on your fingers.
You'd give them kisses with your eyelashes. ·
You were brave like that.
When you step into your shoes,
it makes a terrible crunching sound.
And I start to cry.

You smile, and I know you must feel guilty.
But you have no time for that grief.
You move fast,
too fast for me and the bees.
So we sleep in your shoes,
and wait for there to be space in your hands.
We are with you every step,
even when it kills us.
The next morning I wake up,
and I try on your shoes.
But there's nothing in them but me.
It's funny how things leave us.
Do you remember the bumblebees?

# On Family

## Sis

You walk,
my living heart outside my body,
holding hands and skipping feet.
The best parts of me,
made into you.
Or maybe the worst parts of you,
made into me.
My twin.
Even if I die,
a part of me will live on in you.
And I know you will miss me,
as I miss you.
Every time you leave the room,
I carry you with me.
My living heart.
My forever love.
My twin.

## Seagulls

I miss who we both were.
The way I held you,
and the way you let yourself be held.
The soft of your hands.
Before they knew the sharp of another.
The way you never cut me down,
not even once.
If I was giant,
you were 10 feet tall.
The seagulls,
like me,
loved just the shape of your face.
And I swear,
when you left,
I never saw another bird fly
by your house again.
I miss the seagulls.

## The Earthworm's Savior

It rained this morning.
I stepped onto my porch,
and the earthworms on the cement,
sang your name.
And I could hear,
the water in their lungs.
I knew if you were here,
you would wish
you had a hundred tiny lips.
To give a hundred drowning worms,
mouth to mouth.

My brother,
the earthworm's savior.

## I Am Her Shadow

In God's sunlight,
streaming through the windows
to the cracks of the floor
and frames on the wall,
I move in her shadow.
She folds the blankets
I've known since I was a babe.
My feet stick out now
and my toes weep
for what we've both outgrown.
You don't outgrow sunlight.
We don't outgrow each other.
My Mamaw.
She raised my Papa
and she raised me.
Maybe she raised Gods son too.
Or maybe God himself.
If he is hers.
Then so is the sunlight.
My Mamaw.
She
made the whole sun.

## Mama's Hair

I do my mothers hair
in the kitchen.
Run the comb down her head
so soft.
I have my Dad's hair and his eyes.
But I'm still her daughter.
Still her baby.
I get the tangles out,
gentle as I can.
Don't think about
how she used to brush my hair.
I do my mothers hair
in the kitchen.
Run the comb down her head
so soft.
And that is the poem.
That is the poem.

## Mama's Flowers

I know you bought me flowers,
Mama.
Let me find a glass vase
and fill it with city water,
while my country blood
begs for the well.
Thank you for the flowers,
Mama.
I'll leave them
in our living room,
my bedrooms
got no windows.
Me and those flowers
are both aching for sunlight.
Pretty things die
in the dark.
I loved those flowers,
Mama.
The curve of their stems
and the soft of their petals.

I'm trying to love my soft too.
I breathe and it's all
thorns and sharp.
I'm sorry
sometimes my words cut you.
You're a good Mama.
And I'm trying to be a good daughter.
I miss
those flowers, Mama.
I wish I'd kept them better.
I've got a bad habit
of letting all the wrong things go.

*Althea's tattoo, inked in 2020*

**Papa**

And this
is the sum of things.
I believe in the sun,
like I do my father.
When it shines,
I hear him laugh.
And I bask in the light,
of love so warm,
it burns you.

## This Book is for You, Dad

When I told my Dad
I wanted to be a poet,
I expected him to laugh.
And he did.
"You already are one,"
he smiles.
And I laugh this time.

# About the Author

Althea Davis is a newly published poet in the Columbus, Ohio area. She began writing as a child and never stopped, with the dream of publishing her own book. Her writing has strong ties with family, love of all kinds, religion, and surviving past trauma.

Instagram: @_altheadavis_

TikTok: @writerandweeper